This American Life Sef

(The life of African immigrants in America)
In 5 Essays and 2 short stories

By

Rudolf Ogoo Okonkwo

Outstanding Acclaim for Rudolf Okonkwo and "This American Life."

"Man, you got me there thinking. What you narrated above is the agony most people living in the west go through, even though most of us wouldn't admit it."
- Emeka London.

"I have since withdrawn my green card application!"
- Anonymous

"This article brilliantly summarizes the dilemma of living in a strange culture that offers material benefits but no cultural or spiritual grounding to our youngsters."
- AU Citizen.

"Yeah… It's hilarious, but it's also quite true -which is the tragedy."
-Gbosa Express.

"This is a CAT scan, MRI, X-Ray and Ultra Sound all rolled up in one. So now that we have been diagnosed, let's find a Cure."
— Anonymous.

"You captured the plight of most Nigerians who have sojourned to the US and indeed UK and most of Europe. You will remain a 2nd class citizen and by the time the

rejection starts dawning on you it may be too late as you become too old to make any reasonable response and then you are destitute."
- Nzeman

"Rudolf Okonkwo is sick and tired of the USA-he wants to go home-but where are the resources to aid him on his way back to his village?"
— Anonymous.

"This article is a harsh reality check. It mirrors the life of a whole bunch of us in the diaspora now - and going forward."
- Stan Okey Odume.

"This man just put it together like priest predicting the future of a young man who wants to come to America. Na you *biko*."
— Agbelero.

"The Rudolf trademark; Intellect, Wisdom, Satire, Humor, Comedy, Bitter truth, Fiction all rolled in an amazing cocktail of readability if I am right."
- Anonymous.

"This article is so important that it should be sent to all secondary schools and markets in Nigeria. It is apt for America and true for Europe: Italy, Greece, Spain, UK : even Sweden and Germany. No better place than a functioning Fatherland!"

— Denis Ezieme.

"Rudolph work this out to a really big book, a beg. I have never read any article on any Nigerian website, but the article is all about me and my friends."
— Anonymous.

"OK, for once I give it to him. THIS IS A CLASSIC."
— Danladi Ibrahim.

"This article is indeed a classic.
It also made me laugh my....... to nuts in public.
Ironically, it's so true, even for those of us that are not yet living in America."
—Oye

"Never read your piece before until this one. I am counting my loss. Superb writing. The title could as well have been: This UK Life."
— Tufiakwa.

"Rude Boy,
You're good. You're very good. When I grow up I will write like you.
I tire for this American life."
— Isi-ike

"When I see your write-up or jokes, it reminds me of the fact that Nigeria has lost so many of her brains to brain-drain."

– Anonymous

"Rudolf, you are a comedian. This is film stuff, and with a brilliant team (script writer, producer, director et al) this will have the box office bursting and people rolling off their seats. At the same time the actual story and your heartache will not be overlooked. This is brilliant stuff! Well written. Kudos."
– Ms. Omayeli Odeli.

This American Life Sef
© 2015 by Irokopost Media Group Inc.
Rosedale, NY 11422

All rights reserved. No part of this book mat be reproduced or transmitted in any form or by any means without written permission from the publisher.

ISBN-13:978-0-9768354-2-4

Printed in the USA by 48HrBooks
(www.48HrBooks.com)

Cover page art by Solomon Isekeije

Dedication

To the people who made my American journey smooth – Samson Okafor and Anuli Ezumba Okafor, Pius Airewele and Rose Egbuiwe.

"We don't receive wisdom; we must discover it for ourselves after a journey that no one can take for us or spare us."

    Marcel Proust (1871-1922)

Contents

1. Dedication   page 7
2. Quote   page 8
3. Content   page 9
4. Preface   page 10
5. Introduction   page 12
6. I'll Marry When I want   page 14
7. Saving Mama Udoka   page 22
8. Just Before You Kill Your Wife   page 32
9. This American Life   page 37
10. Our Children Are Coming   page 43
11. A Kernel for a Fowl   page 47
12. The Butcher, the Surgeon and I   page 62
13. Acknowledgements   page 93
14. About the author   page 95

Preface

Every sojourner owes a debt
To the roads, the rivers
And the spirits that pilot the stars.
But the debt that lives in whispers
Is the debt of return.
It's one debt that is never forgiven
Not by bankruptcy
And not by death.
So what happens to the debt,
When the sojourner cannot return?
Does it morph into a myth of thunder subdued?
What happens to the journey
When desires mutate the mission?
Does it trim the wings
And let the treasure be?
What happens to the home
When wants alter the DNA of its bones,
Does it turn into a nursery
For children of the great beyond?
Each sojourner answers these questions
In their own ways.
Some with tears dripping down their cheeks
And some with honey on the edges of their smiles
Whatever your story is
The heels that embarked on a journey
Has earned three privileges:
The right to sing and dance

The power to order the mouth to recall
And the guts to hold up a mirror.

Introduction

I was struggling to snap my seat belt in place without looking like a Bushman but the man sitting next to me in the plane could see the orbs of sweat forming on my forehead.

"Your first time traveling abroad?" he asked. I nodded.

Seat belts in a plane are not different from the ones in cars. But I did not know that because in my father's Peugeot 504 L, we never used the seat belts. It was not because we didn't care about safety. It was just that when nine people are squeezed into a car like that, there is no room for seat belt protocol.

I eventually managed to get it in. I wiped the sweat off my face and buckled up for the dreaded plane's take off that I had been warned about. With my heart pounding, this man who would not mind his business asked me; "Where are you going? What for? When are you coming back home?"

I felt like smacking the man. I was pissed off more by the question about when I would be returning back to Nigeria. I cannot recall now what I said to him but I remembered him telling me that he was tired of living in Houston, Texas, and was finishing plans to permanently relocate to Nigeria.

I doubt if I spoke to him again throughout the flight to London. From London I travelled on to Switzerland. Chances are that he told me things about America that I did not pay attention to. Probably the same kind of things I heard from relations who lived in America and others I met while I was living in London. These were things I dismissed with a wave of the hand before they take root in a mind that was determined to get to America.

Because of that man in the plane and many before and after him, I could not feign ignorance like Andy in the classic Nollywood movie, "Living In Bondage." When Andy found out that his friend, Paulo's much admired get-rich-quick scheme entailed sacrificing his wife to the oracles, he lamented, "Paulo didn't explain this thing very well to me."

This is my little way of finishing the job Paulo did not do well. This is my little contribution to the desire by many to shine a light on this American life.

Rudolf Ogoo Okonkwo
Rosedale, New York City
December 2015

Essays

I'll Marry When I want

In less than four years in America, I have seen more dead men walking than I had seen in all my years in Nigeria. Everywhere I look, I see children of Africa who have become ghosts of their former selves. The noisy ones are sheer empty vessels. The dumb ones are experiencing shock. A distorted image of life and perception had transformed the Africans in America into a pathetic lot. There are more of them struggling to retain their sanity than there are those who are struggling to save their souls. The only gap between their American dream and their American nightmare is their American experience.

One Saturday in March, I watched a Nigerian woman who lived in a high-rise housing complex in Massachusetts assemble her family laundry and bundle them into the laundry room on the 8th floor. The crowded room was full of residents who had gathered to do their laundry. The Nigerian woman noticed that white couples came to the laundry room together; the man helping out in carrying the clothes, sorting them out and subsequently folding them after washing. Only African women had to come alone to the laundry, do all the tasks involved, only to return to their apartments to cook food for their husbands, who all the while were sitting on the couch flipping channels in search of violent sports and naked women.

The African man in America is confused. Those who are trying to be Africans in their homes are forced to be Americans outside their homes, while those who are pretending to be Americans in their homes, are daily reminded by the reality outside that they fall short of that title, in effect, raising so many questions and creating so many conflicts. For instance, is a career minded African wife of an African man, with a 9-5 job obligated to carry out the typical duties expected of an African housewife? When the need arises, who is going to sacrifice the time to take care of family problems- the man or the woman? Who is paying the bills and how much of that translates into veto power in family matters?

I once pointed out this perennial struggle of the African man to an African woman. She instantly barked at me. Her question was, how come when the African marries an "akata" or a "fat white trash", he knows how to behave- how to do the laundry, cook, clean the house, take the baby to the hospital, pick up the baby from the day care, etc. while the wife sits at home watching the Jerry Springer Show. But as soon as he escapes from the American woman, he instantly remembers how to be an African man? Because he got himself a slave as wife?

I met this Nigerian man recently. He had spent a greater part of his 19 years in America working at one nursing home after another. He has become an expert at changing old women's diapers. Nothing is too gross for him to handle. He lives in a huge nice house, one that would make you mistake him for a brain surgeon. And of course, he drives a big expensive car. But deep inside him, the man has died. He had to put up the external appearance to beef up his non-existent self-esteem. Unlike most people who love to care for the old, the sick, and the mentally challenged, this man is there just for the money. His favorite expression is that his paycheck "doesn't smell like shit". In his heart of hearts, he hated every minute of his job. But until his dignity is restored, he cannot in any way function as either a real African or an un-hyphenated American.

But don't ever try to use this story to buy the sympathy of the African woman. Unlike the African woman back home, the African woman in America faces a greater expectation from the African society. She, too, is receiving letters from home. And like all those letters, they are asking for favors, like money for hospital bills, ticket to Germany, school fees, etc. She is under the kind of pressure that a typical married African woman at home would not face. She is in effect expected to be a provider as well as the mother of her husband's children. And in this society where the instruments of law favor women, the African woman is stunned that she has remained downtrodden.

What kind of support does the African man need from the African wife in America? A phone bill that is as long as the River Nile? A credit card bill that runs up and down mount Kilimanjaro? A third car payment for the additional van, the symbol of the soccer mom generation? Or is it the yearly mother in-law visit? Or the bringing over of the wife's sister and/or brother to school in the United States? If the head of the household must bear the full responsibility, what happens to the privileges which the American society does not recognize?

When does one tag an African woman wild? Is it when she threatens to sue him for divorce and take her husband to the laundry, as they say? Or is it when she calls the cops and accuses the husband of attempting to rape her? Does buying Victoria's Secret count? The most intriguing fact about the African woman in America is their class. Whether they are "imported" or "exported", the African woman in America belongs to the best of the best. If they fail to stand on their feet for what they believe in this free country, what hope is there for the African woman at home? Have you heard what follows when, in the heat of an argument, an African woman tells her husband, "This is America and..."

On my prompting, an African friend of mine bought flowers for his African wife. By the end of Valentines Day, the flowers had been squashed to death on the man's body. The woman later told me it was the last time she would ever try to make a romantic candle-light dinner. Shame on you Africans, she said. Where is the love? Is America so full of only Okonkwos? What happened to the Njoroges? I understand when an African marriage fails because an African man wants to videotape himself making love to his wife. But to insist on calling your wife Mama Tayo in America where no woman wants to be old is classic folly.

The last time I checked, the African woman is still trying to be African. She is gossiping about other women and their husbands. She is assessing whose Mercedes is bigger. She is quarreling, even fighting. Have you seen them at baby showers? It is a lioness' den. If you are a man, an African man, you don't want to be anywhere near. Despite America's craze for skinny women, the African woman seems not to be particularly worried. Some punish themselves with visits to the gym. Additional burden, you might say, but so far, Holland Blocks and blouses still fit. But as more and more Ally McBeals of Africa emerge, trouble as huge as yellow skin fever in the 70s brews.

I once asked an African man what contribution would he say he made to the American society after 20 years in America. He snapped, "I did not come here to contribute any shit. I came here to make money." He has a house in his hometown of Mbaino in which he would never spend up to 200 days from now till he dies. He had been sending money home ever since he started working, and the demand has only increased. His children understand bits of his mother tongue but cannot say water without pronouncing the letter t. To him, he is accomplished.

I respect the man's idea of accomplishment. But my idea is a little wider. I want to marry who I want, when I want and how I want. I want to graduate from preaching. I want to advance to that difficult practical level where I have to implement what I preach. I want to try to establish that ideal

African family we have been fighting for. Because that is the frontline of this battle of America, their America.

The other day, looking at America, their America and all these battles that African men and women face in this land, I e-mailed the African woman I hope to marry. In my letter I stated my creed. Here are extracts:

"My dear, I am writing this from the very bottom of my heart. I was touched yesterday when you said I had changed. It wasn't because you were right, rather, it was because I had been debating the very opposite... While a part of me may be half-dead, a significant part is still half born. I don't know what is dying but I do know what is being born. The labor of its birth has been going on for so long. Sometimes, I cry for a stillbirth, rather than an endless pain of labor without any fruit.

"...Sometimes I see myself as firewood. I see myself trapped inside the three-legged metal that holds the pot in the chimney area of the kitchen. I notice the coal underneath me. I feel their warmth- their simmering. I could see Mama picking the grains of rice, washing them, and getting them ready for cooking. But being a very dry firewood, I catch fire. I start burning before Mama is ready. Question: How do I learn to simmer until Mama is ready? And what if Mama doesn't intend to cook immediately? Or she chooses to use the microwave?

"...I am looking at a lot of philosophical questions; what good is a road if it will ultimately not lead to happiness? Where did I come from? Who am I? What is the purpose of my life? What kind of person do I want to be? How should I live? What really matters? Do I want it to be said that I dreamt? Or that I achieved my dream? That I tried? Or that I accomplished?

"I am undergoing a critical search for meaning. I am trying to respond effectively to the forces of nature I face. I try to be principled without being an extremist, flexible without being brittle. I want to be resigned but not uninvolved. But most importantly, I want to love more than I want to be loved. There have been so many beginnings in my life with so few finishes. I feel like a failure when I know that I have not fulfilled the duty that comes with my privileges, especially when I feel it is divine in nature. The responsibilities that come with rights. But most importantly, I am fighting to face faith, my faith; and reason, my reason, equally. Finding the balance for these elements is the very ground of my battle.

"... I do not feel that the danger is that I am changing. Rather, it is that I am not. It would have been a sustainable situation if I was not being told that the only way for me to remain the same is to change... I have vowed to follow this story of you and I to the end. I will juggle my obsession, if that is what it is, with my thought. I will develop my images and hold on to my perceptions. I will maintain my attachments and solidify my clinging. To the world, I may be a one-person army fighting a cause of a lifetime. But there will be peace in my grave if once in a while you remember that I love you."

In other words, I will marry when I want.

Saving Mama Udoka

The two of us waited outside his office for over half an hour. She did not say a word to me despite three attempts on my part to start a conversation. Not even when I dropped the ultimate discussion generator: this country sucks. She looked timid in her flowery gown. The gown was sewn in an obsolete Nigerian fashion. She appeared to be in her early 20's and very weary of the American society. I could see that from the way she reacted when he walked out of his office to peek at those waiting for him. She quickly jumped out of her seat and sent out a loud "Good Morning, Sir." Looking at her, it was obvious she was very anxious. More than thrice, she adjusted her gown to make sure she looked good. Once she brought out a pocket mirror from her handbag and checked her face. With a trembling hand, she applied light make-up to spots she felt hadn't received adequate make up. Merely observing her gesture, it was apparent this meeting was very important to her.

I was there to find out from him how the Nigerian community was doing in his city. I was doing an informal study on love and marriage – the trends and travails. He is a well-respected community leader; the type people at home call "big man". He owns an employment agency that employs a lot of immigrant workers. Men and women searching for a start in the New World always accost him. His position gives him a pivotal insight into several issues affecting the lives of people. He does not just manage a business in the human services, but he also manages people. And that was why I chose him for this study.

She went in first to see him. Twenty minutes later, she walked out with a wide smile on her face, her anxiety all gone. She waved goodbye and walked away quickly and happily.

When I went in to meet him, I asked him what he did that put a smile on the woman's face.

"I offered her a job," he answered.

"Why would a job be so important to her?" I asked.

"Because she has never worked in this country for all the three years she has been here. Her husband kept her at home and turned her into a baby-making machine. She has given birth to three kids in three years. She doesn't go anywhere with her husband and she doesn't participate in community activities. She just stays home with the babies. She does not drive, so she cannot go out alone. There is no reliable public transportation system where she lives, so she is more or less dependent on her husband who works at night and comes home tired. For three years, she has depended on her husband for everything. Now, her mother-in law has come to live with them and she is stepping out for the very first time."

"The coming of her mother-in-law must be a great relief for her and her husband," I said.

"Not really. It is now the beginning of a new conflict. Her husband is threatening to send her and the children back to Nigeria if she defies him and goes out to get a job."

She was a college student at the University of Nigeria, Nsukka, when he came from America and asked her to marry him. She was twenty-two years old, while he was 38, though at that time, he told her he was 33 years. She wanted to come to America, even though she did not know why. All her beautiful young friends were marrying young men who lived abroad and she too wanted to marry one. The alternative she knew would have been to marry a trader, the idea of which she hated. She had resisted marrying other men from her ethnic group who were based in other foreign countries, and her parents had begun to panic. She had been told repeatedly how difficult it would be to find a husband after she graduated from the university. Her mother had warned her about many young girls who were coming of age and would soon steal the spotlight from her. "You see Aunt Ebele," her mother was fond of saying, "she used to be stunningly beautiful." She made *inyanga* for all the men who came to marry her, now, see how miserable she is." All these stories scared her. She capitulated.

To say that her husband is insecure is an understatement. He firmly believed that if he let her step out, there were young men who would take her away from him. So he vowed to keep her away from public view. To keep her busy, he made sure she was pregnant, almost all the time. To his friends who showed concern for her, he would remind them that he has been taking care of all her needs without complaints.

"When the kids are grown, then you will complete your education." That was his standard answer to her demand to finish college. Privately though, he would tell his friends that her schooling would only resume when she got older and less attractive. She yearned to understand the society she found herself in. She was eager to make her own money, no matter how little and be able to assist her parents and siblings without having to beg. "You should be happy you have a husband who hasn't turned you into a money making machine. Haven't you heard of other men who specifically married nurses and brought them to the U.S. to slave away? I provide you with all your needs and this is how you show your gratitude?" her husband would scold.

The first time he came to visit her at Zik's Flat hostel at UNN, she was rehearsing her lines for Shakespeare's Romeo and Juliet. She was Juliet in the school play. Four years later, she wondered how she seemed to have abandoned all her ideals, her vision of life, love and happiness. Her dream of a young Romeo who would love and cherish her had since been turned upside down. And even the 'bliss' of being in America, she could not lay claim to. She thought of her fall from a bubbling chickito to Mama Udoka and could not fathom what had happened to her. One morning, after a talk with her Nigerian neighbor in their dilapidated apartment, she decided to find herself a job.

Thirty minutes later, I stepped out of his office and found her by the bus stop waiting for Bus 261. I walked up to her and introduced myself. And she began to talk....

I am a girl trapped in a woman's body. My life is what some will call 'girl, interrupted'. When I was a teenager, I believed I had star qualities. I was exotic, sprightly and inviting. I envisaged myself being something more than just the woman next door. It was my dream to contribute to my society. I grew up playing up my best features and ignoring the worst. I modeled my life principles after my makeup regimen. I blurred and bled my makeup layers. I avoided strokes, swipes and straight lines. I used a little of the same blush; I gave drama to the eyes. I avoided black eyeliners and mascara. When I applied makeup, I did so in natural light.

His idea of fun on a weekday after work is to sit in front of the television with the remote control, channel surfing and on weekends lie on the couch all day long snoring. After the kids go to bed, he would watch "Girls Gone Wild" videos. For me, not being able to go to the theater or see a movie, I would sit and read Dame Barbara Cartland romance novels. He hardly reads. I believe the last book he read (fiction or otherwise) was in college in the early 80s. He has this bookshelf at home filled with books on business and finance, knowledge he is yet to put to use; that is, if he ever acquired it. When he sees me reading, he feels threatened. "Don't get yourself worked up over things you read in books", he would say. "Reality is very different from what the books say."

When he is done watching naked women flouncing around, he would come looking for sex by asking if I wanted some. I do not mind sex if only he would be romantic about it and a little adventurous. But what I get is the same boring thing night after night, year in and year out. He would not even make love in the morning or afternoon. It was always at night with the lights turned off. Woe betides me if I sought out sex from him. He did not think good Igbo women asked for sex. He also thought it very disrespectful for a wife to initiate any sexual contact. But, if there is anything I have learnt from all the years of sitting at home watching soap operas, Jerry Springer and Oprah, it is that talking about one's emotional anguish is the first step in healing. I have tried to get him to loosen up, but he is so set in his ways. When would he realize that there are other ways of making love besides the "missionary style." Things he loved for me to do for him and to him before we got married, all of a sudden are taboo in this house. Now when I do those things for him he says "only prostitutes do things like that." I feel so sexually frustrated. Love making in this house seems to be only for procreation.

As a young girl, I dreamt about marrying a man who would show me love. A man who would take me on long walks along narrow paths, hold my hands, caress me softly and rub my hair, lay with me on green grass, whisper sweet nothings into my ears, kiss me passionately under the full moon and make me his princess. I dreamt of being a valued member of my family, a voice in the decision making process. I had thought that my husband and I would be partners in life's long journey. Little did I know that I would be turned into "that woman" or just "Mama Udoka", whose only life function is to clean the house, take care of the kids, pick up after my husband and have sex when and how he feels like it. I waste away without being appreciated or respected. In short, I am just a doormat.

I love theater. I love movies. But since I came to this country, I have not had the opportunity to explore any of these interests. He would not let me. He frustrates all my attempts to maintain friendship with other women my age. He claims they would spoil me. He would not even let me watch BET or listen to Hip-Hop music. He says Tupac, Destiny's Child, TLC, Ja Rule and other similar artistes promote decadent forms of entertainment. Mind you, this is the type of music I grew up on. He listens to Marvin Gaye, the Cool and the Gang, Osadebe, Sir Warrior and other musicians of the 60s and 70s. We would fight in the car when I tuned the radio to more modern and contemporary channels. A break from his Osadebe cassette tapes would not be permitted.

Once in a while, I like to eat out, or order in. When I first came to the U.S., he took me out every other week. Now, like my sex life, that is a thing of the past. Even when I am ill, I still have to cook for the family, while he lies on his couch with his remote control. It is bad enough that I have to cook when I am ill, but he still has to make outrageous demands, like saying he would not eat any soup that is more than two days old, or that he would not eat rice kept in the fridge. I also want to try other kinds of food, like American dishes, Chinese food and even Thai and Indian food. But oh God, he is so fixated on his African dishes. When I prepare anything other than Nigerian food for the kids and I, he is quick to remind me that I am wasting money. "Where a poor girl like you picked up this sweet mouth, I do not know, and it is not like you are even bringing any money to this house," he would grumble.

I know there are many in our community who would say I am a bad woman when they hear me talk like this; that I am badmouthing my husband. But mine is a cry for help. My mother's generation was brought up with the notion that silence in the face of emotional abuse and unhappiness is a virtue. I owe it to myself and to my children's generation to begin the process of changing all of that and healing. I don't think my husband is necessarily a wicked or evil man and that he is doing all of this just to punish me. I think that our conflicts are a result of a generational gap and the way males are brought up in Nigeria. My decision for now is to put my foot down, do what I know is right and get him to take a whole new look at life.

People who have known him for a long time have told me he was not always like this. They said he was a kind gentleman when he first came to America. I tend to believe them for he is nothing like his parents, which is a story for another day. I was told that his first wife whom he married in order to get his green card really dealt with him. She literally made him use his toothbrush to clean the toilet, I hear. On a daily basis, the two of them fought themselves to a standstill, but he put up with her for fear of not getting his green card. The six years they were together totally transformed him, a classmate of his revealed. Now, he is a shadow of his former self – drained – emotionally and psychologically. He is absolutely afraid of anything that reminds him of her.

Yet, I do not think I should let myself be a punching bag for whatever flashback he is experiencing. I, too, have my life to live. The sins of another woman should not be visited on me. I have tried to be as different from his first wife as possible in order to make him feel secure and comfortable. I have even given up wearing any decent clothing. He calls them provocative dressing and unfit for a married woman. Even the negligees I wear just for him are evidence of low moral standards. One summer day, on the anniversary of our wedding, I wore a strapless dress and he freaked out. He ordered me to remove the dress. I resisted. That was the first of many times that he hit me. Previously I would just sit there and cry. These days, I hit back.

Over the weekend, as I push my Stop and Shop carriage filled with dirty laundry in a black trash bag to the local Laundromat, I hear a car horn. I take a quick glance from the corner of my eyes and quickly see a rather handsome black guy in the car. He looks vaguely familiar, but I don't stare or stop to speak with him for fear either my husband or one of his friends would see me. My heart is thumping and I cringe at the thought that perhaps this guy knew me in Nigeria in my "babe days". To think that anybody who knew me from my University days would see me pushing a shop cart with Udoka sitting in the carriage, his nose dripping with mucus sliding towards his mouth and both hands stuffed with fried plantains, I cringed.

As soon as I start working, I will pay for driving lessons and get my driver's license. No need asking him to teach me how to drive for that would be like knocking on the horn of a toad. When I earn a little money, I will buy myself a used car. Only then will I be truly free in this land of the free and the home of the brave. In the meantime, I will continue to sit here and wait for Bus 261.

Just Before You Kill Your Wife

There are so many reasons to kill your wife, a wife, any wife. I knew this even before I got married. So I am not going to debate that with you after five years of marriage.

If I want, I can call you stupid – stupid for ignoring that warning written on the gwomgworo 911 lorry, plying the Onitsha-Nsukka road that says, "Fear Women." You did not fear women. You stubbornly went ahead and got married. I wanted to say, "*Ntoo,*" but I didn't because what I intend to say here is serious, and I do not want to lose you.

So let's jump to the reasons why you may need to kill your wife.

She makes more money than you do. Okay, it's not really the higher earning power that pisses you off, it is the spending. She does not hand the paycheck to you so you can decide what it should be spent on. Okay, I know. You don't really want her to hand the money over to you, you are not that kind of bushman. In fact, you don't even care what she spends it on. You just don't want her to demean you in the manner that she spends the money. Yes, like putting up a storeyed building in her father's compound when your parents still live in a mud house. After all, you brought her to America and paid her school tuition as well as the mortgage while she studied nursing. You did that by driving a taxi. You deserve more respect.

Ha, she came from a well-to-do family. Yes, the elite high society family. You got to marry her because you live in America. America nullifies status and allows you to cross the social line. You lied to her about what you were doing in America. But you have since resolved that. You thought she only married you just to come to America, but you have had three kids and you have forgotten about that fear. You have begun real estate agent classes, so you will soon be wearing suit and tie. But now, her family is telling her what to do. She is listening to them. They are treating you like trash. Yes, especially that evil mother-in-law. They won't back off from your marriage. Everyone is still mocking you. You brought her to America, and this is the thanks that you get.

You did not tell me, but I heard it through the wide-open grapevine. She is following other men. She did not tell you that you were not satisfying her in bed or that you are too old for her. But she is following younger men, some half your age. No, it wasn't the *akata* men that made you mad, it was other Nigerian men who now tell everyone that your wife is "Mrs. Donatus." It breaks your heart and makes you feel impotent when you know you are not. You have even gone out of your way to buy books and films just to help improve your sex life. But it looks like it is too little too late. It doesn't seem like she will come back to you.

Didn't I hear you say that she isn't beautiful anymore? You said you needed to find younger women to make you feel young again. But being as stubborn as she is, she won't let you be. She keeps following you around, threatening to divorce you and take you to the cleaners. You have said to her that if it were in Africa, you would have married an additional three wives. I hear you. You need to do something to stop her. The nagging, the fighting, and the threat to half of all you worked very hard for. I hear you. The insurance business you have been building for the last twenty years.

I heard that the judge awarded her $3000 in child support money every month. He also gave her and the kids your home. Add that to the $3000 she makes in a month and you will see why she has so much money that she throws around with one boyfriend after another. Meanwhile, you make $4000 a month and after paying her the money that she squanders, you are left with $1000. It is not enough to pay the rent in your small apartment. Not enough to begin your life again. Now, she doesn't even want you to have visitation rights. She lies to the judge that you are a threat to your own children, just like she lied that you make more money than you actually do. It is provocative. I know.

She said she went to university in Nigeria. You brought her here and had hoped to send her to nursing school. She could not pass even the CNA class. She has failed nursing entrance examination four times. She is so dumb that you often think she needs help crossing the road. She is good at watching TV. That's it. She won't even keep the house clean. She is a liability you need to get rid of as safely as possible.

There are many reasons to kill your wife, a wife, any wife. I bet you can come up with more and more.

For now, I want to tell you about an armed robber I admired so much. He was 63 years old. He walked into a bank and gave the teller a note saying that he was robbing the bank. The teller gave him all the money she had on her station and pressed the red button. The man walked out of the door and handed the money to the bank's security guard. He waited for the police. They came and arrested him. Upon investigation, it was discovered that earlier the man had given out all his valuables and had returned his apartment key to his landlord, telling him he would not be coming back. When asked why he did what he had done, the robber said he could only get minimum wage jobs and was tired of living hand-to-mouth. He said he felt it would be better to spend two years in prison, with free food and free medical care and by the time he is out, he is qualified to collect social security benefit.

That is the robber after my heart.

Just before you kill your wife, decide on where you will wait for the police. I don't want to hear that you ran into the bush or took off in a car with your kids. You embarrass me by that kind of action. You know they will catch you so why don't you do the honorable thing and act like you are ready for them.

So before you kill your wife, pay off what you owe Igbo organization of your city, including the one for the Igbo House Project so that if you die in prison they may send your body home, which is necessary for you to reincarnate. Oh, never mind. For a moment, I forgot that those who committed *alu*, abomination, do not reincarnate.

Just before you kill your wife, return that Nigerian movie you borrowed from me. You don't have to pay off your credit cards, or car payment, but at least, settle the pepper soup woman at our joint. She needs that money to continue to serve our community while you are cooling off in prison.

Just before you kill your wife, remember that it will become official that O. J. Simpson is a descendant of the Igbo if another Igbo man kills his wife in America.

Just before you kill your wife, picture your children coming to the gate of that state penitentiary to pick you up after you have served 30 years. Imagine how you will feel when they open the door of that Limo and let you in. And I hope you will smile wildly when they take a selfie with you and say, "Dad, thank you for killing Mom."

Just before you kill your wife, remember your father had many good reasons to kill your mother. But he didn't.

Hopefully, you are thankful for that.

This American Life

You come to America, young and dashing, on a full scholarship, finish school, get a great job, marry a glamorous spouse, have cute children, and retire at a young age with a great pension, portfolio and posture.

...And live happily ever after. Yes champ; rub it in.

For the rest of you, life abroad is a crest of trajectories.

You come into America, by air, by sea, or via a midnight sneak-in across the Mexican border; fooling the Minute Men and Lou Dobbs all at once. You come to school, to join your spouse, to work after winning the Green Card Lottery, or to raise your hand at the airport and claim persecution in your own country because you are a Mormon as well as a leader in MEND.

You behold America the beautiful. The triple-decker burgers and the giant cup of coke and cars that are wider than your village road and you wonder what took you so long to get here. You get on with schooling. For now any cheap school will do. You study the things people who came before you say brings money – the things Americans do not want to study- to prepare you for the job Americans do not want to do. You hear nursing, bloody, nursing. You say, bring it on. You get on with marriage - convenience marriage- discovering that you married three persons at once; the person you thought you married, the person your spouse really is and the person your spouse becomes because you got married in this America. For work, you do anything for a dollar; cut meat in fast food restaurants, drive a cab, guard the parking lot of company executives younger than you, even care for the disabled, breaking your back to pay the bills.

Then reality hits. The dollar is not adding up. There's more going out than there is coming in. Time is running. Letters, emails and phone calls are enveloping you from home. School is done; where is the job? Your accent is a problem. Racism is real. You're finally squeezed in. Then comes a Corporate job at last. Work place politics really sucks. Meanwhile, the American spouse is gone but your residency is established. Now where do you find someone to marry for real? A blind date? E-harmony.com? Town conventions? What of picking up someone from your village? But these are all packages which content you cannot ascertain. Somehow, you settle with one. Honeymoon over, now what is the state of the marriage? First mission accomplished, now what next?

You start a house in your village. A big house. You sink in any money you can get. Some of it goes to the building of the house but most of it goes to your family member who is supervising the construction. It costs more than it would to buy a comparable house in America. You are afraid to calculate how many days you will sleep in this house in your lifetime. You say, *Tufiakwa*. It will not be your portion. You need to do it not just because everyone is doing it – your daddy is demanding it. He's asking you to wipe away the shame on the family's face.

Your daddy dies. Your dentist extracts a tooth.

Then America begins to reveal itself quietly. Oh tribalism again; discrimination at the workplace. Your head touches the virtual ceiling for immigrants. You now understand affirmative action. Kids come but housemaids are tagged slavery, who will care for them? Now you have day care, mortgage, after school sport activities, mid-life career crisis, more phone calls from home, and marital problems. If only some of these can wait. You can call marital problems by its real name- money problems entangled with control problems, decision-making disagreements, tasks and privileges, status problems and in-law problems. Maybe you will stay home with the kids. Maybe your mother will come and help … and incense your spouse.

With caning banished, you raise teens with your hands tied to your back. Marital problems persist because as your fortune falls that of your spouse rises. You have done your calculation. Something has to give. You try selling real estate. You prepare taxes. You sell insurance. You run out of contacts. You buy cars from the auction and ship them home. You get duped by friends and family. Nothing is adding up.

Fast insurance fraud deals? You try other businesses on the side, but total dedication is needed. You quit your job entirely and start a business. Cleaning business. Staffing business. Medical equipment. Home Health business. Escort service. Oh, these taxes, running costs, government paperwork and lack of patronage by your own people.

Marital problems persist. You wish you had married the lover you left in Nigeria to come to America. You take the divorce option. Half of your wealth is wiped out in the process. Now rages the battle for visitation rights, alimony and child support. You're estranged from the kids because of the stories your spouse made up against you to win custody. But you keep paying up. You have no option. You start afresh. A new apartment. Maybe a new spouse? No, that can wait. Your classmate at home becomes the CEO of a multinational company. A chieftaincy title follows and you wonder what happened to you.

You consider a fast 419 advance fee fraud deal. You remember those acquaintances still doing time in US prisons. You hold off. You dream of a contract from the government at home. You write a proposal. You get in touch with an old classmate who has done well.

Home looks attractive. The people you left behind are doing better. You conveniently forget the majority who are not making ends meet. You are overwhelmed. High blood pressure is diagnosed. High cholesterol. Heart problems. Another tooth is extracted. You join the gym. You stay away from garri and Farina. You join a church. You can be a pastor too, but you don't like that lifestyle of pretending to be what you're not. Life is no more fun. You go home, dabble in business, in politics, in entertainment.

You are burnt. You return. You start afresh.

No, you won't take the divorce option. You will manage. You will live like roommates, until the kids are grown and are out of the house. You will wait for retirement. You need just ten more years. At 56, with social security plus pension pay and 401K, you can go to the village, if kidnappers permit, and enjoy your old age. And start afresh. Maybe marry anew. Maybe teach in a college in Nigeria. Yeah! You register for a PhD with an online college.

Your Mummy dies. Your dentist extracts another tooth. Your doctor suggests knee and hip replacement. Your shrink prescribes Prozac.

In spite of your *wahala*, the children grow. The girls do well in school. The boys go from four-year colleges to two-year colleges, in- between gang membership and police troubles. The boys marry White girls. The girls marry African-American guys. You're glad the girls did not get pregnant out of wedlock. You thank God the boys did not throw a coming out party to announce that they are gay. One lives in Arizona and another in Hawaii. Your house is empty, calls come on holidays only.

It is now time to really go home. But what about managing the diabetes? Do you trust the doctors at home to handle your dialysis? Your medication cocktail will be hard to find at home. Daddy and Mummy are dead. You have to make new friends again. The ones you used to have are now strangers to you. Your spouse refuses to go with you. Spouse cannot deal with the sound of electric generators, untreated well water, Afor Igwe meat without an FDA inspection tag.

You retire. You sell the big house and move into a small condo. When you cannot wipe your behind, you go from the condo to a nursing home. Your children are too busy to have you share their homes. They visit every presidential election year. Once again, you think of going home but no, it is rather too late for that. The twelfth tooth is gone. You now take more pills than the teeth in your mouth.

So you stay until your autopsy is ready. Your townsfolk contribute money to ship you home. As your coffin lands in Lagos, your relations who have gathered to receive you for the last time mutter in-between breaths, *Tufiakwa*. Yes, the same *Tufiakwa* that you said the time you read the article called 'This American Life'.

Oh, about your kids, well, some of them went home with your body. Those few times you cleaned your bank account to take them home paid off. They watch as sand lands on your coffin. One even remembered how to say, '*Kedu*'. They leave soon after. They will come back one more time – when they accompany your ex on the final journey home.

Our Children Are Coming

Contrary to what many Nigerians at home think, living abroad has numerous downsides. Many who migrated abroad find out after a while that they do not belong to either the society they left at home or the new one they inhabit abroad. Aside from all the problems associated with surviving in a foreign land, those abroad miss a valuable opportunity to grow up with their extended family and friends they made in the early stages of life. Often, some simple pleasures of life, usually underestimated, come together later in the course of our adventure abroad to make life awful, if not miserable. I have heard an elderly Nigerian complain that his greatest loss was his inability to marry his high school sweetheart as a result of his decision to emigrate. By all accounts, the most frightening downside of living abroad is the possibility of losing our children to the new society.

The Nigerian child born abroad is at best a hyphenated Nigerian. More often than not, these kids are not Nigerians in both nature and nurture. The forces of the society where they were born into usually frustrate every attempt by parents to raise then up as Nigerians. As these children grow, parents are at a loss as to how to imbibe in them the things they had while at the same time giving them the things they did not have. It is the greatest dilemma of life abroad.

What has been proven beyond reasonable doubt is that, no matter how much parents tried, Nigerian children born abroad who had no chance of forming a strong attachment to Nigeria are most likely to see their host country as their home. This leaves most parents in an unpleasant position where they face the possibility of spending their retirement years alone in Nigeria or in a nursing home abroad. It is one prospect no Nigerian parent wants.

Many parents are currently trying various approaches to the problem with little success. There seem to be a consensus that the only way to make the children born abroad develop an attachment to their parents' home country is to have them live for a while at home or visit often. When to visit home and how long to visit is still not clear. When to send the children home and for how long hasn't been ironed out.

The logistics of sending a child home are enormous. There is the question of who will take care of the child at home? There is the anxiety over insecurity at home and lack of basic healthcare facilities. But more importantly, there are questions about the very nature of the knowledge today's Nigeria will be able to impart on these kids. No doubt, the Nigeria of today is a far cry from two decades ago. How much of what rubs off today's Nigerian youths do parents want their kids to pick up? Are the admired values acquired by these parents few decades ago still obtainable in Nigeria?

Currently, a good number of parents send their children to Nigeria for their high school education. The reasoning behind this is that it is manageable at that age. Most parents cannot emotionally afford to send a toddler home even when they have reliable relations. And by the time a kid has finished high school abroad, it is much more difficult to get their cooperation. Also with persistent strikes and closures, college education in Nigeria has become unappealing.

There are other formulas being tried out. In some cases, one of the parents opts to go home to raise the kids. This could only work in few cases where the financial and marital health of the couple is strong. There are cases where regular visits to Nigeria for holidays is the approach being adopted. But again, very few people can afford this. Some parents in big cities try to create a home away from home. They establish networks in which Nigerian children relate with one another and in some cases attend language classes, seeking means to encourage courtships leading to marriage.

Despite all these efforts, the success rate of children born abroad identifying with the home country of their parents is relatively low. They seem to be overpowered by the pressures of their host country's mainstream culture. The most likely direction of these children is the adoption of the lifestyle of their peers in an effort to belong. This often ranges from minor irritations like tongue piercing to major concerns like interracial marriages. What follows are decisions that greatly reduce the chances of the child ever returning to Nigeria. Which means that most Nigerian parents abroad would either retire in a nursing home abroad or alone at home. That is one unpalatable possibility that stares many Nigerian parents in the face.

A look beyond the first generation born abroad presents a bleaker picture. For even in those rare cases where the parents succeeded, there is an even slimmer chance that the second generation of Nigerians born abroad would succeed in stopping their children from completely assimilating into the new society.

What this means, then, is that Nigerian parents abroad are basically fighting a losing battle. One hundred years from now, their lineage at home would be forgotten entirely. Their epitaph would read like those sold into slavery 400 years ago. The big houses some are currently building in cities and villages across Nigeria would be taken over by relatives left at home. Many who are already seeing this possibility and cannot live with it are beginning to regret the very day they went to the foreign embassy to seek a visa. Some, though very few, have returned home to face whatever challenge they encounter at home.

In a recent discussion of this issue with my friend, Obinna, he came up with a classic macho plan to resolve the problem. His plan is to marry one wife in America and another in Nigeria. When he is ready to go home and retire, he would have a family at home to spend his twilight years with. Next week, I will visit Obinna and essentially discuss his plan with his girlfriend, Ify. I can't wait to hear what she thinks of Obinna's plan.

Short Stories

A Kernel for a Fowl

After years of pursuing men, you believed in a man being dropped right into your arms. It was the Almighty's purpose for you. And that was how you met him. It validated your belief. It hardened your heart to everything else anyone was saying, including Ihuoma, your girlfriend. From then on, everything else was undue mocking of tired people. And coming from Ihuoma, who had not fared any better in the hands of men, you had no problem waving it aside. You had no fear that, like she said, you might be cracking a kernel for a fowl.

You were a nurse, a degree-holding Registered Nurse. You never forgot that you ought to be rich. You worked round the clock. Every shift American nurses declined, you would accept. Holidays and all, you were available. In fact, you loved the holidays because you got paid double the time. And at sixty dollars an hour, a double meant more than a new hairstyle. It meant a day at the spas, a visit to Bloomingdale's and another bottle of Agent Provocateur.

You drove a big BMW, an SUV model. Most men who had the opportunity to get close were intimidated by your confidence and poise. Those who were not, who dared to approach you with brilliant pick up lines, you had doubts about their sincerity. You could not figure out if they were coming to you because of your hard earned money or to take advantage of the residency status which you had earned as a nurse.

It wasn't long ago when he told you that you belonged to him. You assumed that it meant he belonged to you. You were an African, but you now you live in America. You cook with the microwave and you bathe in the bathtub. You fetch no firewood and you draw no well water. You eat hamburgers and not *foofoo*. You wear jeans and not a *buba*. No proverbs were created around computers, ipods and GPS systems, so you accepted that it meant all proverbs were suspended. You had crossed seven seas and seven rivers. You had left behind the seven idioms of the seven shrines of your homeland. You were now in the land of the free and the home of the brave. All old things had passed away.

So you allowed him to etch a tattoo down your waistline. He tattooed you that first night he made love to you. You let him draw a big stop sign. He painted it red, too. When you wore a tank top, the red sign showed at your waistline. Your panties often split the sign into two. Further down, he wrote a special note. He ended it with an exclamation mark. His note read: Private property – do not trespass. Scorpions on guard, ready to sting objects as little as index fingers - men beware! Then you lay there for three hours as he drew a scorpion. You did not mind as he scraped off some pubic hair to find space for its tail.

He asked you to tattoo him too. But you were no tattoo artist. You were just a nurse. You told him not to worry. You did not need to draw your face around his penis to be assured of his faithfulness. When he asked you what you would have drawn, you lied to him. You did not tell him you would have drawn a long rose stem. Instead, you said to him, "I would have drawn a gun and simply written beside it, in capital letters, BANG." You knew you were lying. But lying had become part of your life. Your true self had not taken you anywhere.

You were not always like this. In fact, when you came to America, you carried with you, like a little shell, all the norms you learnt at home. You dared not look a man deep in the eyes. Your Mama taught you to carry yourself with grace. Growing up in Enugu, you were able to resist the pressures of your peers. You still hear your mother's voice. "Uzo, don't be like those loose girls who are spoilt and are not good for marriage." But her voice became fainter as each day passed. You had managed to confine her voice to a small cubicle where you stash things of the past.

If only Mama could see you, she would not believe what you had become. You had become a grown woman. A woman, ten times the woman she was. You knew what you wanted and how to get it. You did things that she could not imagine in this life and maybe, in the life to come. Somehow, you had learnt to please yourself. Sometimes you worry that you might be in a rush to recover the years you spent trying to please Mama. You do not regret those years. Without the restrictions, you probably would not have won the scholarship that brought you to America. But you were happy to throw away all inhibitions of the past.

He was the one who opened your eyes. He was the one who led you to places you did not know existed. In moments of bliss, you did not fail to remind him that he spoilt you. You liked to be spoilt. You liked to be pampered. You liked to be worshipped. You liked your man to think of nothing else but you. And you had succeeded with him. Like a tortoise, you had made him desire you. He desired you so much that he had agreed to lift the earth onto your head. Your only challenge was finding a place for him to stand as he did that.

You were not just a taker, you were also a giver. And that was how you met him. You were doing a graveyard shift at the trauma center of Union Hospital in Lynn, Massachusetts, when paramedics rushed him into the hospital. A Latino gang member shot him right inside his barbershop/tattoo parlor. You were assigned to him after surgery to remove a bullet lodged in his thigh. A foot higher, the bullet would have shattered his manhood. When he came out of surgery, it was the first thing he said to you. And you laughed.

You cared for him that night. You cared for him like he was your brother. You continued to care for him in the days that followed. He had nobody around. His two brothers and sister all lived in London. You knew this because you bought the phone card and dialed the numbers for him as he informed them of his ordeal. They called. They sent him flowers. But they were too busy to fly to America. His parents in Nigeria were too busy with local politics to come too. His friends came when time permitted. But you were the one who was always there.

When he was discharged, you continued to visit him at home. You cooked and baked. You made meals, soups, and porridge. You helped him clean his house. You dressed his wound. You even helped him run his barbershop before he finally sold it. The gunshot he said, was just a warning. But for you, it was a sign you had wanted to see for so long. At first you did not know why you were doing those things. But you were sure they were the right things to do.

It had been a while since you last did something because it was right. You had learned that, in America, because it was right wasn't a good reason to do anything. In America, experience had shown you, people did things mainly because it felt good. You had paid a heavy price before you learnt this. The scars on your soul, the patches on your emotions and the wrinkles in your smiles were constant reminders.

Caring for him felt good. Considering where you came from and what you had been through, it did not make sense. But deep inside your heart, it felt good. That was how it started and blossomed into a love affair.

***

Everything was going well until his mother came to visit. It was his mother who unmasked you. She was the one who told him who you really were; that poor *wawa* girl whose mother sold bean balls, *akara*, in front of Chief Obiozo's house. Yes, it was you.

His father and Chief Obiozo were friends, thus he was a friend of Chief Obiozo's children. He visited Chief Obiozo's house many times. You were a secondary school student then, some seventeen years ago, and so was he. You admired him. From the boys' quarters where you and your mother lived, you saw him drive in several times with Obiozo's children. You were jealous when you saw beautiful girls in his arms. You wished you were one of those girls.

When they threw parties, you peeped through your little window and wondered how great their lives were. But you remembered what Mama told you; that you were given a different destiny - whatever that meant. You knew that your place was lower than his, even though you were in the same class, but different schools. He was attending the elite College of Immaculate Conception, Enugu, while you were at the lowly Idaw River Girls Secondary School off Agbani Road, also in Enugu. In spite of your different stations in life, you knew about boundless goodness that surpassed all imaginations. You knew this because your father, a driver for Chief Obiozo, died during the Biafran war. He was Chief Obiozo's aide de camp. You were told he gave his life for Chief Obiozo to live. Faced with a bleak future, Chief Obiozo took you and your Mama into his house. He contributed to your education and you were almost like his daughter.

"Almost" you would say, because you were not part of Chief Obiozo's children's parties. You were not friends with their friends. If you were, you would have been in his life before now.

When Chief Obiozo was not home, you were more of his children's servant than their friend. You remembered one night, during one of the wild parties Chief Obiozo's children threw, when Kenny, Obiozo's first child, called you in to perform a chore. You could not remember what the chore was. But you remembered going into the kids' wing of the big house and seeing a living room full of beer bottles and cigarette butts. Half–naked girls were lying on the carpet. You remembered seeing him there. You remembered him because he came to your rescue when one of Obiozo's children grabbed you and started fondling your breasts. You did not like what he said that night. You did not forget it, either. But you were still grateful that he rescued you. In fact, you have rationalized what he said so much that you have convinced yourself that he only said it to protect you.

"Leave that *ngbeke* alone," he said. It had the same effect on you then that "leave that nigger alone" would have had on you today. Only that now, you knew you would be grateful to a white man if he said that and saved you from possible rape in the hands of another white man. That was how you rationalized it and compartmentalized it. You packaged it and keep it where you store things of the past.

Then, his mother came and revealed them all.

You were kind to his mother, too. When she came, you took time off from work. You drove her around and showed her places. You shopped for her; bought her expensive jewelry and clothes. You took her to every mall and every outlet in New England. She only needed to look at an item twice before you picked it up for her. You took her to the museum. You took her to Faneuil Hall and New England Aquarium. At Boston Wang Theatre, you saw the Broadway show, Les Miserable. You rode on the Boston Duck Tour. You saw her laugh as the duck became a boat in the river and a bus on land. She marveled at that. She called it an American wonder. You were glad she liked it because she did not like Salem, the Witch city. You gave her a good time.

You thought things went well. When she was leaving, you gave her money too. You were not trying to bribe her. You were not even acknowledging that the path to a man's surname often started with the approval of his mother. You were doing it because, on so many levels, it felt right.

She seemed grateful for all you did for her. After each outing, she gave you a little more crayfish. Then she gave you garri. By the time she gave you *ogiri*, you were sure you firmly had her in your camp. Not that it was your goal all the while. As you accompanied him to the airport to drop her off, she surprised you when she gave you some yards of lace and material for a wrapper. Even though it was the cheap *aba na anya* material, you were very grateful. As you hugged her for the last time, you called her Mama. It wasn't the first time you called her Mama, but this time, it came out with a deeper meaning.

***

By the time his mother visited, you had known him for over two years. You had seen him grow from nigger-wanna-be to a well-balanced black man. It started with the gunshot wound but you had a lot to do with the final outcome. When he owned the barbershop, he also drove a cab. The two occupations placed him in direct contact with the most violent people in the society. You helped him in his transition. You bought him the equipment he needed to become a DJ. It was what he wanted. He did that for a little while but business was not booming. He abandoned that too.

You encouraged him to go into nursing. He resisted many times. He was afraid of math and he hated biology. You made him take the North Shore Community College LPN entrance examination. He failed thrice.

He said he wanted to be a computer network administrator. You paid five thousand dollars for him to attend a training institute. He completed his courses. He studied hard and obtained his A+ certification. By the time he was done, the computer boom had fizzled out. Those who were surviving were those who got in not for the money but for the love of computers. He got in for the money and when the money was not coming, he put away his chips.

Finally, he settled into real estate. He became a realtor. He wore a suit and tie, expensive shoes and went about seeking people who want to buy houses. He was good at it. He had a sweet mouth. And it helped that he was handsome. It made wives encourage their husbands to listen. Many listened and he sold many houses. You agreed with him that he had found his calling.

But then, all his friends and acquaintances who had good credit and could afford the down payments had all bought houses. His options began to narrow. You helped him buy two houses. It was a small business of renting for him. A cushion. You also helped him start a staff recruiting agency that sent nurses and direct support staff to nursing homes and group homes. For a long while, you and your nurse friends were his core base of nurses.

As you helped move him towards more stable and responsible career choices, you also noticed his stabilization. It was gradual. He reduced the number of days he went to the gym and began to see himself beyond the puffiness of his muscles. You noticed the changes from the nature of the haircuts he was getting. You could also see from the size of the pants he wore. As he slid from the hardcore hiphop worldview to a middle class black outlook, the size of his pants reduced. His pants also climbed up his butt. You were glad that your man was coming home. You were hopeful that he was settling.

***

But as soon as his mother left, you noticed a change in him. He wasn't as open as before. You asked him once what was eating him and he said he was being pressured by his mother to get married. You tried to console him. You tried to tell him all parents were designed to think like that. You tried to tell him that your mother had also been pushing you in the same direction.

You did not tell him, "Hello? What's the problem?" You did not say, "I'm here!" No. You encouraged him to listen to his mother and yet to make his own decision.

When he suddenly announced that he was going home and would stay for two months, you did not have any worries. After all, it had been a long time since he was home. You volunteered to help him run his businesses, but he refused. That surprised you because you had been helping him in the past. But you did not read too much into it. Not even when his agency stopped calling you for work. You did not care because you were never short of work hours anyhow.

He went to Nigeria and called you once. You did not hear from him again. One month, two months, three months. You were worried. You sent him an email but he did not respond.

You visited his house and there was no sign that he had come back. You visited his staffing agency office. It had been closed. You made enquiries. You spoke to his friends but nobody seemed to know anything.

Even though you missed him so much, you gave him his space. It was very painful as your birthday came. Last year, you traveled with him to Disney World. It was there that you marked your thirty-fourth birthday and he celebrated his thirty-sixth, which was two months after yours. You missed him but you also knew in your heart that he was God's gift to you. *Agaracha*, wanderer, you told yourself, must come back.

Then four months after he went away, during your birthday party, someone gave you a strange gift. It was an envelope with a business card inside. You looked at the business card. It was his. It showed his name, new address and phone number in Worcester. A note on the back of the card said he had returned from Nigeria with a nineteen-year-old wife and they both live in Worcester.

You stormed out of your own party like buttocks stung by a vicious ant. You entered your car and drove to Worcester. You could not recall stopping at any traffic light. You could not remember paying any toll at Tobin Bridge. The last time you were in Worcester, you had come with him to attend a pre-wedding party of a Kenyan friend at Lucky Dog nightclub.

You got to the address and saw his Mercedes car parked in the driveway – a car you made the down payment for. You sat outside his house and watched, while your blood boiled inside. From the window you could see two figures moving around the house. You called the home number on the card. You saw him walk towards what must be the phone. He paused at what must be the phone's caller ID. He did not pick it up. You waited for two minutes. You called his new cell phone number. He did not pick that up either.

You sat in the car for a long time with your eyes focused on the house. As tears began to build up, you saw the two figures inside what looked like the living room area. He held her hand and they began to dance. The scene broke goose pimples all over your skin. You called again, this time dialing * 87 first to conceal your phone number. He walked toward the phone but still did not pick it up. You saw them swinging into what looked like the bedroom.

You wished you could be invisible. You wished your phone was a gun. You wished you had enough gas to pour round the house and set it ablaze. You wished you could invoke the tornado of 1952 on the house. You wetted your fingers with your saliva and rubbed your eyes. You were not dreaming. You called again. This time, the male figure did not walk toward the phone. He switched off the light as the two figures gently landed on what must be the bed. You knew exactly what would follow. You have been there.

You started your car and drove away as erratic as a sliced worm, wondering amongst other things if he had given her a tattoo too. And if so, what her tattoo might say; Scumbag?

As you drove home, tears trickled down your eyes. Every mile away from Worcester, its seven steep hills fading behind, you imagined the undertakers preparing your first love for burial. This is one funeral you will not attend. You had waited for eternity for those tears to flow. Now you feared it would flood Lake Quinsigamond. But weeping was all your soul needed to be free.

At Tobin Bridge, across the Mystic River of Massachusetts, the spirits of those who could not bear loads like this besieged you. They said, "Stop the car. Climb out. Take a jump off the bridge. Immerse your tired body into this cold water. It will cool your soul." There were many voices. They were loud, cluttered and making eerie noises across the cantilever truss. You heard a voice like that of Charles Stuart. His murdered pregnant wife sobbed in the background. You heard a splash as his body made the 115 ft plunge into the river, causing receding ripples just as Boston police circled his home.

You slowed down your car. You pulled up by the emergency lane. You clicked the door open with your tear-soaked hands. The night was chilly. You looked out and saw darkness as creepy as a monster's claws. Suddenly, the voices stopped shouting and began to whisper in seductive tones.

You put your foot out and it felt unsteady touching the frozen bridge.

From afar, you heard police sirens singing a dirge. They were coming toward you. They were driving up fast. You ducked into the car like a scared snail burying its head in the shell. You started the car and drove off in a panic. The voices jumped into the car with you and began to call you a coward. You assured them you were not a coward. You debated with them. They insulted you. You continued to drive, fidgeting and frightened. You turned on the radio to interrupt the voices. On the radio, the alternative rock band, Failure came on. They were singing, "The Nurse Who Loved Me."

"Say hello to everything you've left behind

It's even more a part of your life now that you can't touch it

I'm taking her home with me, all dressed in white

She's got everything I need; some pills in a little cup

She's fallen hard for me; I can see it in her eyes…"

Those were the last words you heard before you smashed into a pavement a few yards off the bridge.

The Butcher, the Surgeon and I.

On a sunny Thanksgiving afternoon, I stood in the kitchen of my Southern California home, heating a quart of oil in a saucepan and mixing onions, peppers and a castor seed condiment, *ogiri*, in a soup plate. It was the last *ogiri* in the house, one of the food items I looked forward to replenishing when I got the chance.

Warming inside the oven was a turkey delivered by caterers, and four pieces of plantain I had roasted earlier. I poured the hot vegetable oil into the mix, wishing I had the palm oil used by Nkanu women to make the tastiest plantains on the sidewalks of Enugu. Ideally, I would have added the vegetables into the saucepan, watched them sizzle and stirred the mix with a wooden spatula, but not in this house.

In order to reduce the smell emanating from the dish, an aroma that the initiated find pleasant but others find disgusting, I quickly covered the plate with a saucer. Some of the smell however escaped so I quickly grabbed a fan and began to direct it away from the window to the backyard where my wife was playing with our grandchildren. The fan was not doing a good job so I hurried upstairs to the bathroom to pick up a can of air freshener. When I returned to the kitchen, I found my soup plate in the sink.

"Even today!" I said to my wife as she leaned on the fridge, frowning. "On Thanksgiving day, on our 40th anniversary, you could not even indulge me, Georgina?"

My two sons Cal and Williams were standing at the bar, holding their noses. My daughter Brenda was busy opening the windows and spraying two cans of air freshener at the same time. My oldest grandchild, Cal Jr., looked at my face and asked in his eight-year-old voice, "Grandpa, were you planning to eat that thing? It smells like rotten cheese."

The boy had my broad nose, big ears and oval face. His hair was curled and dark like that of the Nkanu warriors of years past. His brown eyes skipped two generations to look like those of my father. In spite of the resemblance, I felt I was alone in this family – cut off from everyone.
"You all should leave grandpa alone," said Brenda's six-year-old daughter, Brittney. "All grandpas do the things they like. That's what makes a grandpa a grandpa."
As she spoke, her blue eyes shone. With her long face and rosy cheeks, she looked a lot like Georgina in her kid picture. "That's my girl," I said as she ran across the kitchen into my waiting arms.

I picked her up, kissed her forehead and rubbed her long hair. I swung her around while singing the chorus of the Temptations' song, "My Girl", as we made our way to the living room.

I overheard Williams say he thought the caterers brought some fabulous Thanksgiving meals.

"As he gets older, he gets worse," my wife said to the children. "If I let him have his way, he will start behaving like his butcher father and this house will be a refuse dump."

"What do neighbors say when they see you in the morning?" Cal asked.

"Nice flavor you had going last night," my wife said. "What was it you were cooking? Goat meat?"

"Do they really find the odor pleasant?" Williams asked.

"Of course not," my wife said. "They make fun of us."

"But Mummy," Brenda said, "you used to love those odd things about Dad."

"For a while, odd is exotic," my wife answered. "But if it lingers, it becomes disgusting."

"But some of that will always be part of our heritage," Brenda said.

"The problem with idealism is that it pretends not to have any limit," my wife replied. "I've got to the limit of idealism and there is no where else to go."

I showed Brittney the people in the pictures lining the walls of the living room.

"This is your great grandfather," I said to her pointing at my father's black and white picture. "He was a great man when he was alive."

"What did he do?" Brittney asked.

"He taught me how to be a surgeon before I went to medical school," I answered.

I overheard the conversation in the kitchen.

"I am happy I did not buy into this whole African thing," Williams said.

"Not even with the Obama phenomenon?" Cal asked.

"I have never been tempted to," Williams said. "I find it hard to embrace backwardness." For a moment, Williams sounded like I did when I first came to America.

I heard someone turn on the sink's waste disposer.

"Who's this?" Brittney asked, pointing at my mother's picture.

"She is your great grandmother," I said.

"Was she great, too?" Brittney asked.

"She was a great home maker."

"What does that mean?"

"She made everyone around her feel at home."

"Oh."

The screeching of the disposer drowned the chattering in the kitchen. I carried Brittney over to the entertainment center and turned on the stereo.

"Ready to dance with grandpa?" I asked.

"Yes."

I put her down as the music of the Temptations filled the room. I held Brittney's hand. She twisted her body around as we began to dance.

At the end of "My Girl", a few seconds before "Just My Imagination" began to play, I saw Cal Jr. standing at the base of the staircase sucking his thumb.

***

I have practiced obstetrics and gynecology in Los Angeles for over thirty-five years. I often performed surgery on pregnant women whose babies were days behind their due dates. Some of the babies I delivered have graduated from medical school. I have three homes. The first is in Nkanu, Nigeria, the second is in Cerritos, California and the third is in Enugu, Nigeria.

I take vacations twice a year. I usually spend the winter in sunny Africa and the summer in Europe, Asia or Latin America. I have done so every year for the last twenty-nine years. As I got older, historic sites in other parts of the world fascinated me less. I have seen them all. Their once lovely smells have now turned into the stench of their brutal histories. I am no longer an innocent tourist who sees the fresh paints and not the graffiti they cover. I see ghosts hanging on rooftops of palaces. On the skies above the edifices, I see blood hovering around the clouds like a dirty rainbow. At the foot of great pillars, I see footprints of slaves and ponds of sweat lost as they hauled the stones that built those monuments. It troubles me. It stopped me from seeing the fluttering wings of the pigeons. It stopped me from buying souvenirs for those who could not see the real thing. It stopped me from enjoying the delicacies served at restaurants near these historical sites.

I have not always been like this. I believed in Western civilization. It saved my life. I once vouched for it. I once thought the Enlightenment was the greatest gift the West gave to the world. I believed it was what differentiated the West from many other societies, including my hometown, Nkanu. In my quiet moments, I believed I would bring enlightenment to my own people. That was why for the last five years, I have been considering returning to my hometown permanently. I felt it would be a good place to retire. My decision has nothing to do with the transformation the practice of medicine is going through in America. It is irritating, but I am too old to care. I pay my malpractice insurance and as much as possible; I protect myself with a whole lot of paperwork and still manage to make a good living. My strategy is to do little direct patient-doctor work. I am a consultant at the University of California teaching hospitals. Young doctors surround me most of the time. But I am also tired.

Part of the reason why I am homeward bound has to do with my children and my wife. Georgina, my wife of forty years is now like one of those monuments of Europe. She is of high value to our visitors, but for me, she is just there. She no longer inspires me to dare. Our lives, our home and our acquaintances in Cerritos are all in her image.

Except for when I travel to Nkanu, she is in total control of my life.

Last Christmas, amongst our visitors was a colleague of mine, Dr. Ikedife, from Malibu, California. I went into the kitchen to make plantains with my famous sauce. I peeled eight plantains in quick succession. I rubbed light vegetable oil and salt on each one and placed them inside the oven for forty-five minutes during which time they became brown and soft inside. I brought out onions I had kept inside the refrigerator for twenty minutes. I peeled them without tearing up. I diced the onions into tiny cubes and also chopped red

Mexican peppers. When the oil was about the right temperature, I poured in the mix. It sizzled, letting out a mixture of aromas. White smoke quickly engulfed the kitchen. Georgina was so disgusted with the pungency of the *ogiri* that she poured the sauce into the sink and splashed water on it. She did not care that Dr. Ikedife was watching.

"Never when we have company," she said after she saw how gloomy her action made Dr. Ikedife and I.

On this Thanksgiving Day, I did not invite Dr. Ikedife. I thought my children and grandchildren were family and did not count as company. Evidently, I was wrong.
...
I met Georgina at the State University of New York at Buffalo, New York. It was 1968 and interracial romance was uncommon.
"What's the meaning of Okons?" she asked, the first time we met in an English 101 class. I had to explain to her that Okons was not my real name. It was an abbreviated form of my full name, Okonkwo.
"Why did you abbreviate your name?" she asked.
"To make it easy for Americans to pronounce," I said.
"If Americans had a problem with your skin color would you bleach your skin?" she asked.

That was how our relationship started. For a teenager from tropical Africa stuck in freezing Buffalo, she was my fireplace, keeping me warm with her smile, her energy and her love for life. No wonder we had two kids, Brenda and

Cal, even before I graduated from Medical school. Her studies were interrupted by the kids' arrival. But she eventually graduated from the school of pharmacy. We moved to California in 1975 where we had our third child, Williams. She stopped practicing pharmacy many years ago when she began helping manage my medical practice. These days she does voluntary work at the Museum of Science in Pasadena, California.

Georgina has aged. Contours of wrinkles line her face. Under her eyes are bags of tears that were never shed. I once offered to pay for a facelift. She did not speak to me for weeks. When she was younger, men skipped work just to soak in her beauty. She had blonde hair that once reached down to her shoulders. She stood on tall legs; like a flamingo. She was one surprise I never expected. At college, those resentful of our relationship called us Queen Elizabeth and Idi Amin.

I wasn't blessed with good looks. But I had a well-built frame that even my worst enemy acknowledged. My bones were strong, and connected a network of sturdy muscles developed from years of felling trees with axes, climbing up the hill with buckets of water fetched at the village stream, Ngene, and slaughtering goats.

Yes, before I became a surgeon, I was a village boy who knew how to sharpen and wield a knife. Before I opened books on anatomy and physiology, I had opened up the carcasses of hundreds of goats. This surgeon who delivered babies by caesarian operations had in the past gone into the bellies of goats with almost the same skills. Before I spent years in medical school, I had learned the importance of each body part on my father's butcher's table. The elders of Nkanu did not joke with their goat meat. The kidney was important to them the same way the placenta is to a pregnant woman. The gall bladder must be cut off with great care lest it burst and ruined the taste of surrounding parts of the meat with the bitterness of its bile. Every bone of a goat was accounted for. Even the intestines were cleaned out and shared. I had single-handedly cut up many goats given to the village as marriage gifts in my last two years at home. I had spread out each body part delicately on banana leaves. The ribs were sliced up according to the number of families in our clan. The waist, carved out in the right manner, was reserved for the daughters of the village. Elders inspected the process like attending physicians, frowning at errors and barking at misplaced portions.

I was headed for Afor Ogbete market to begin a career as a butcher when I won a scholarship to study in America.

Be it Oye Olisa, Afor Igwe, Nkwo Nnewi, Oye Agu, Afor Nnobi, or Nkwo Agbaja, whatever market there was East of the Niger and beyond, my people dominated the butchery business. We monopolized it. When we went in, others went out. I had done my apprenticeship at Afia Ogbete where my father was a well-known butcher. After school, on weekends and on holidays, I would go to my father's stall to help him. I made my mark on goats amidst vultures and hordes of flies.

I used to get to my father's stall early in the evening, take off my school uniform in a kiosk behind the stall and put on my khaki shorts and jumper. I would tie my white apron, now stained to an unnamable color with goats' blood round my waist, wash my hands and step up to the cutting table. My father would move out of the stall in order to give me room to take over. He often took time off to sniff some tobacco as lines of Nkanu women formed in front of his stall.

"How is our favorite school boy doing today?" the women would demand as I performed my preparatory rituals that included washing the knives, covering garbage bins, spraying disinfectants and air fresheners. Some love-struck women would say, "Show us those sturdy muscles of yours."

I used to smile. The arm muscles would pop up as soon as I grabbed the first lump of meat.

My father's competitors murmured that I attracted these women with voodoo. They called on the women to come to their stalls and get better deals, but the women would stay in line even as competitors screamed the price-busting slogan, "*Mgbuka! Mgbuka!* Buy one and get one free." My father would nudge me to reduce the portion of meat I cut for some of these women customers. I was about to take on cows when my scholarship letter arrived.

My only brother, Ezeagu, was bright at school, too. Just like me, he learnt the skills required to run our father's stall. He also learnt to study hard, sometimes burning the proverbial midnight candle quite literally with his feet in a pail of water. When I left Nigeria before the Nigeria-Biafra civil war began in 1966, he was still in secondary school. He fought in the war as a child soldier, working with the intelligence group called the Boys' Company. These were children who crossed the enemy lines and sent information back to the Biafran side. He got shot in his right leg after a captured Biafran soldier under torture blew the cover of the Boys' Company. The bullet lodged in his bone causing him to limp. He could not go back to school after the war. He lost the desire to study. I tried to encourage him with materials and funds but he suffered severely from posttraumatic stress disorder. He returned to our father's stall at Ogbaete market and continued the legacy.

For years he was the head of the butchers association of Ogbaete. Now he manages our family compound. Though I ensure he is well taken care of, he still insists on living the village life. He loved to climb palm trees to tap for the sweet frothy white wine.

The pogrom that led to the civil war made me believe that black people were heartless butchers who deserved no place in civilized societies. I lost two uncles in Northern Nigeria's pogrom against the Igbo. They were butchered by knife wielding Hausa men. My Nkanu people worked with knives too. But they didn't go about cutting down innocent people to settle political quarrels. I lost both my parents during the civil war that followed. My father died of kwashiorkor, a disease that normally kills malnourished children. His death brought shame to all of us because he had a protruding stomach before he died. Before the British occupation, people with an affliction like his were dumped in the evil forest and left to die. My mother was raped by occupying Nigerian soldiers who overran our hometown at the early stages of the war. She later died of heartbreak. I did not want anything to do with black people until Georgina convinced me otherwise. At first I thought she was one of those who allowed white guilt over slavery to overshadow their reasoning. But she persistently made her point ever so gently that I began to reconsider.

"Do you understand what happened at the Berlin conference," she asked in those early days.

"Yes. The Scramble for Africa," I answered.

"Do you really understand it?"

"Yes, I do." I said quickly, trying to avoid a lecture.

"It is like having a meeting in Mecca and the Emir of Kuwait declaring that the whole of North America, Canada, the United States and Mexico were his personal property. That was what King Leopold of Belgium did."

"And so?" The question had come out of my mouth before I realized that I had invited a lecture.

"He basically claimed a land that was over eighty times larger than his kingdom and brought several diverse peoples with different cultures and languages together as one country," she said. "No input from the people. Just like that."

"But African people should be over that by now," I said.

"Yes, they tried. Patrice Lumumba tried. But what happened? The same Europeans murdered him and in his place they installed their puppet, Mobutu."

"You are correct."

"It was not always the making of black people," she said. "There were always powerful external instigators and willing local thugs in whose hands black people were often helpless."

...

When I first went back home in 1979, Georgina was the one who insisted on the trip. She liked it then. It was a relatively prosperous Nigeria, quiet and promising. We returned each year, the last being in 1984, a year after the military took over power again.

We had a peaceful Christmas holiday at Nkanu. Our kids enjoyed life in the village setting as well as the days we spent in the city. We arrived at Eko Meridian Hotel in Ikoyi, Lagos, for the last leg of our journey on Boxing Day.

On the last Saturday of the year, Georgina and I got a call from Dr. Ikedife, who was spending his holidays at the Lekki beach area of Lagos Island. He had asked us to visit him at his newly completed house. We climbed into our rented car, pulled out of Adetokunbo Ademola Street and set out on our way.

The roads were free of vehicular traffic. The notorious Lagos Island traffic was not to be seen. The drive along the Island was as smooth as a drive on the Los Angeles freeways on Super Bowl day. The ghettos of Maroko and Ajegunle with their shanty houses were off the radar. Lagos Island had modern bungalows, expensive mansions and an extensive well-graded road network. Populated by top government functionaries and rich businessmen, including foreign nationals, the lawns were manicured the way they were done in the wealthy parts of the western capitals.

"Maybe we should build a house here and retire to its quiet neighborhood," Georgina said.

The gentle breeze from the beach was cruising in and out of our car through the open windows.

"You mean it?" I asked.

"Yes," Georgina said. "It is beautiful here and very quiet."

"I told you that the military boys are cleaning up the country."

"You won't say so if you were among the young students they executed at that beach recently."

"They were drug traffickers," I said.

"They don't deserve death."

"Africans need a strong hand that will mold them into a civilized people."

"Look at what you're saying."

"I'm serious. Some people must pay a price for the transformation of a society" I insisted.

"Will you pay a price if asked to?"

I thought about Georgina's question as we passed through Eleke Crescent where many foreign embassies were located. If anyone was blindfolded and dropped there, they would never imagine this was somewhere in Africa. The architecture in these parts looked foreign; the flowers on the perimeters were tropical but were groomed with a touch of western expertise. The Crescent stood in the shadows of the

Marina where modest skyscrapers provided proof that the multinationals have long arrived.

We headed to Lekki Road along the Lekki-Epe Expressway. We were halfway across the Mobil petrol station when a roadblock confronted us. There were two cars in front of us and the occupants were sitting on the ground by the roadside. They had their hands on their heads. Standing beside them were half a dozen heavily armed soldiers. They flagged us down, signaling us to stop. I stepped on the brakes.
"Step out of the car, Mister," screamed one of the soldiers.
"What's wrong?" I asked.
"I said step out of the car."
"Anything wrong?" I asked again.
"Are you deaf?" the soldier asked looking agitated.
I stepped out.
"You mistress too," the soldier demanded.
"That's my wife," I said.
"*Na you sabi*," the soldier dismissed in his heavily accented Pidgin English.
"What's going on?" Georgina asked.
"Honey, please step out of the car," I said.
She stepped out.
"What's wrong officer?" I asked.
"Go sit down there," the soldier yelled.
He walked away.
I stood there with Georgina looking at a young couple on the floor with their hands on their heads. At the other end of the road was an elderly man with his driver sitting on the asphalt sidewalk.

"What's going on?" Georgina asked me.

"I don't know. But I will soon find out," I said.

The soldier soon returned after conferring with his superior sitting in a kiosk beside the roadblock.

"So you two are too good to sit down?" he asked.

"There is no seat here," Georgina said.

"I get it," the soldier said. "Your white butt is too pretty to sit on an African ground?"

"Let us sit down," I said to Georgina.

"I am not sitting on the ground," she said firmly.

I stooped a little. The soldier stormed toward us. I dropped my knees and found myself kneeling on the ground. I tried to pull Georgina down but she pulled her hands away.

The soldier got to us in three steps.

"Lady, sit down!" he yelled.

"I'm not sitting on the ground," Georgina replied, unfazed.

In one swoop, the soldier kicked both her feet, flinging her to the ground. Georgina landed on her backside. She let out a cry and then a series of sobs.

"Put your hands on your head," the solider ordered. "Bloody idiots!"

We obeyed.

"What is wrong, officer?" I asked. "What did we do wrong?"

"You broke the law," the soldier said.

"What law?" I asked.

"Don't you know we are in a war?" the soldier asked.

"What war?" I asked.

"The war against indiscipline," he answered.

"So what law did we break?" I asked.

"Law against indiscipline," he answered.

"What does the law say?" I asked.

"That you should not drive on Environmental Sanitation Day," the soldier said. "You should be home cleaning your house."

"But we are staying in a hotel," I said.

"And so?" the soldier muttered as he walked back to the kiosk.

I had heard about the sanitation day but had never experienced it. It was part of a series of edicts the military had put in place to bring order and structure to society. I was an initial supporter of the reforms because I saw how people were lining up at bus stops and at the post office and I liked it. It looked more and more like a civilized society. I had dismissed criticism from the elite that the military were abusing civilians in the course of instituting these transformations.

The soldier returned. He asked us to form a straight line. And we did. He ordered us to walk up and down the expressway picking up litter. When we were done, he asked us to open the trunk of our cars and dump the thrash in there. Georgina walked beside me. She cursed all the way. She was loud at first until the soldier confronted her.

"If you curse one more time, I will throw you into the bush," he warned.

Then, he burst into a tirade.

"This is not the World Bank. This is not the United Nations. This is not one of those fucking institutions where your country humiliates developing countries like ours. This is

Lagos. Your cowboy president can wake up and bomb sleeping children of Libya but he cannot do shit here. This is Lagos. We said we do not want to owe you guys anymore. We want to pay you off. And you said no, we must owe you. What kind of nonsense is this? We want to be free of your debt. We want to determine our fate but hell no. You want to keep us tied down. So much for 'all men are created equal.'"

When he was done, Georgina's curses had watered down into whispers.

I noticed that some cars were allowed to pass the roadblock without the occupants being asked to step out. Most of these where military vehicles, painted dark green, with military brass sitting in the well-upholstered backseats. Others were civilian vehicles with federal government number plates. I saw few private vehicles too with what seemed like very important personalities in the back seats cruise through the roadblock without so much as a second look from the soldiers. A thought came to me when one of the occupants of a newly stopped vehicle was taken to the kiosk to make a call. Thereafter, he was allowed to drive off.

"Officer," I called out.
He turned around and looked at me. He did not say a word.
"Could I make a phone call, please?" I asked.
"To whom?"
"Brigadier Ikedife is waiting for us at his home," I said. "I want to let him know we are delayed."
The soldier blinked repeatedly.

"Brigadier who?" he asked.

"Brigadier Ikedife," I repeated.

He hurried up to the kiosk and conferred with his superior.

"Who's Brigadier Ikedife?" Georgina whispered.

"Dr. Ikedife's brother," I answered.

"Do you know him?"

"No."

"Do you have his number?"

"No."

"What will you do if they allow you to call him?"

"I will call Dr. Ikedife."

It was a gamble I needed to take because the soldiers were not relenting and Georgina's skin was beginning to turn red as the sun emerged. We held our breaths as we watched the soldier confer with his superior. Minutes later, he returned.

"*Oga, make una dey go,*" he said in Pidgin English.

Georgina refused to follow me home ever since. As her faith in Nigeria and anyone's ability to rescue it faded, mine increased. She never returned home with me even after I had built a mansion in the exclusive Government Reserved Area of Enugu. It was an edifice, a manifestation of wealth that would have made my father yell my grandfather's title name, "*Aku rue uno.*" Nothing I did could convince Georgina to give Nigeria another try.

"I've turned you into an African extremist," Georgina said the last time I raised the topic.

"What do you mean by that?" I asked.

"My prayers were answered," she said, "but by then I had started a new prayer."

I had wanted to repeat the cliché about being careful what you prayed for… but I held off because Georgina hated clichés. Her greatest strength was in knocking down truism.

"You bought what I was selling," she said to herself.

"Georgina, please look at it this way," I pleaded. "I still have life in me and can still do some good. But if I stay here, I'm heading straight for the nursing home."

"You can still do some good here."

"But nobody really wants me here or even needs me. I'm replaceable. There are thousands of people like me here. But there, my little contributions will have a multiplier effect."

"What about your family?" she asked. "Why will you choose to abandon them? Is it for fear of the nursing home or this unknown need over there?"

By the 90s, our kids had grown up and left home. Brenda is a doctor practicing in Alaska where she lives with her husband, also a doctor. Cal is a pilot with Air France. He is married to a French air hostess and they live at Long Island, New York and also in Paris. Our last child Williams is a struggling actor in Hollywood. They all stopped going to Nigeria with me when their mother stopped. Not even Williams, who lives nearby, showed up at our house in Cerritos during the holidays. They have all moved on with their lives and once or twice a month I get a phone call from Brenda who would often share brief anecdotes of my grandchildren with me.

If anybody had been abandoned, it was I. And as my father used to say, he who others have rejected must not reject himself.

In 1999, I began a free medical mission to Nigeria. I got together doctors, nurses and medical supplies and for two weeks we traveled across Eastern Nigeria providing free medical services to the rural folk. During each visit, I look out for what I could possibly do if I returned to Nigeria permanently. I still dream about bringing that enlightenment Georgina used to talk about. It was in that spirit that I gave my support to a contestant for the kingship title in my hometown. This was the first contest since the rule was changed to stop making the succession hereditary; as was set up by the British colonial power. I supported the candidate who promised to eradicate the Osu caste system that tagged some citizens free born and others slaves. The slaves were denied full rights of citizenship. It was a controversial and emotional issue that made the traditionalists angry when my candidate was named the king-elect.

Georgina knows about my medical mission to Nigeria. I thought it would touch the humanitarian spirit in her. But she does not care. Our home in Cerritos is a beautiful one-storey building. We have a visiting housekeeper, a gardener and can afford any service we need. Our dog, Mannie, is as old as Georgina. The once energetic American pointer hardly barks anymore. It does not even wag its tail when I come home.

***

Mannie barked three times on Thanksgiving Eve; each time for when the doorbell rang and each of our kids arrived with a bouquet of flowers. We saw our grandchildren for the first time in three years. Brenda had two, Brittney and Stephen and Cal had one, Cal Jr. Williams, I suspected was gay. He came with his 'friend.'

Cal's wife had not changed much from the way she looked on her wedding day some eight years ago. She still had her smile and walked with the same elegance. If I had never seen old air hostesses, I would have declared that air hostesses never aged. Maybe they age slower than other people. I get along well with my daughter-in-law. She radiates courtesy and still has her sense of humor.

"Is the air in the first class cabin really different from the air in the coach," I once asked her.

"No, Dr. Okons," she said. "The air in all the cabins is the same. The only place where the air is different is in the cockpit."

"Why is that?" I asked.

"Because pilots fart," she said.

"Everyone farts," I said.

"Sometimes," she said. "But pilots fart all the time."

If her pilot husband was not within hearing distance I would have discounted that.

Brenda's husband was a lot like me. As a doctor, he had an unobstructed look at the ins and outs of life. He must have adjusted to accommodate my daughter, who is not different from her mother.

He once cornered me at the balcony upstairs and asked.

"Dr. Okons, what is the secret to a long happy married life?"

This was before the incident in the kitchen.

"It is simple," I said. "Do no harm, keep the pain secret and keep away from every seduction."

"Is the answer in the oath?"

"Well, it is like the oath," I said.

"The Hippocratic oath?" he asked.

"No. The other one."

"Which one?"

"The one they call a vow," I said. "You know the difference between an oath and a vow?"

"No," Brenda's husband replied.

"If you violate an oath, you lose your license."

"Aha."

"But if you violate a vow, you lose half your estate."

It was our first heartwarming get-together in years. Our home was lively. Kids were running around, making noise and breaking things. Dinner was served just after the first football game ended and the second was about to start. The Cowboys and the Seahawks again divided the family. Everyone, but Brittney and I were on the side of the Cowboys.

Assorted dishes covered our formal dinning table. Occupying the center was the turkey. It stood out like a fountain surrounded by flowers. There was stuffing, glazed ham, mashed potatoes, peas, carrots and green beans. There was also cranberry compote, gravy, rolls, creamed corn, sausages, strawberry truffle and chocolate cake. Even though every inch of space on the table was taken up, I missed my plantain and sauce.

"This family has come a long way," I prayed. "With tentacles all over the world, may we give back some of the great things in life that we have received through our Lord Jesus."

The Amens I heard were very few. There was definitely nothing heard from the spot where Williams and his friends were sitting.

"Why can't we do this once a year?" I asked, afterwards.

"We cannot fly down here every year," Cal said.

"Why?" I asked. "Have they stopped paying pilots well?"

"It's not about money," Cal said.

"So what is it about? Fear of flying?" I asked.

Brittney smiled.

"Forget it," said Cal.

"We can rotate it," I said. "We can visit any of you in turns."

I looked at my wife and saw her roll her eyes.

"Where will that leave your endless trips to Africa in pursuit of who-knows-what?" she asked, the sarcasm evident in her voice.

"I want to go to Africa too," Brittney said. "I want to visit Madagascar and the Lion King countries."

Sitting all around the dining table in our formal wear with chandeliers lit up above, ours was a picturesque family. Looking back to where I came from, I could see I had indeed come a long way. But looking forward to where my family was headed, I feared it wasn't my destination. Maybe it was the way it should be. But nothing had prepared me for this; getting where I had always wanted to be only to yearn for where I started.

"I will host the next get together," Cal said. "We can meet anytime in our house in Long Island."

"Why not Paris?" Brenda asked.
"If you all are up to that, so am I, hey" Cal said.
"My passport has expired," Williams chipped in.
"Then renew it," Brenda riposted.
"We will work out the details after dinner," I said.

As prearranged, my children's spouses and their kids went out to see a movie after dinner. I had wanted to be with wife and children alone as we discussed my future plans. I was seriously considering spending more time in Nigeria in pursuit of my philanthropic goals. There was also talk about getting a political appointment in the health ministry.
"In the course of human events, there comes a time when a man must answer to his father's name," I began as soon as the front door closed.
"This is going to be interesting," said my wife. "It has transformed from there comes a time when a man must use his tongue to count his teeth to there comes a time when..."
"As opposed to using his teeth to count his tongue?" Brenda interjected.
Carl and Williams all laughed.
The eyes of my children looked like those of kids waiting to hear their father's will. I ignored the snide remarks because all I had said was that I was at a juncture in life when I needed to take stock of my life. I continued.
"You have all grown to be secure and responsible adults," I said, scanning their faces. I made sure my eyes focus more on Cal and Brenda.
"No proverbs, please," my wife said.
"But Mummy, you used to love them when we were small,"

Brenda said.

"Used to…" Georgina pointed out.

"I will be going to Nigeria on Sunday. I'm exploring career opportunities over there" I continued.

"Why?" Cal asked.

"He is afraid of staying here and ending up in a nursing home," my wife said, her disdain once again seeping through.

"Where do old people end up over there in Nigeria?" Williams asked. He was looking at his mother for an answer.

"I don't know," my wife said.

"Like I was saying, I think I have something left in me to give and I think giving to those who have little to nothing is the best gift there is," I said.

"While you're at it, tell the kids about your name change," my wife said.

"Dad, you changed your name?" Cal asked.

"Yes," I said.

"To what?" Williams asked.

"To Okonkwo," I said.

"Oko what?" Williams quizzed.

"What's wrong with Okons?" Brenda asked.

"I don't know what it means," I said.

"Wait a minute," Cal said. "But that is your name and our name."

"Yes," I said. "It was a mockery of my real name."

"Which is what?" Williams asked.

"Okonkwo," I said.

"Does that mean I have to change my name?" Williams asked.

"You don't have to unless you want to" I assured them.

A long silence descended on the meeting. It was the type of silence that seemed to say this was a much more serious issue than we had thought.

In the middle of the preface to my talk I got a call. It was from my nephew in Nigeria.
"Excuse me," I said to my family. "This is from Nigeria."
They shrugged.
"Uncle," my nephew said. "There is trouble."
"What happened?" I asked.
"The abominable," he said.
"What is it?"
"Ezeagu is dead."
"What?"
"He was murdered."
"By whom?"
"By the opponents of the king-elect. They said they were getting back at you for funding his election."
"When did that happen?"
"Yesterday."
"Where?"
"He was tapping a palm tree for wine when they came for him," my nephew said in-between sobs. "They surrounded the palm tree and waited for him to climb down. He tapped his palm wine and descended from the tree carrying in his hands a gourd of fresh palm wine and his climbing rope. He shared his wine with the men who had gathered around him, each drinking from the gourd itself. Then they seized him. Their leader brought out the knife tied to his waist and cut off his head. They laid out banana leaves under the same

palm tree cut up his body into small pieces as if they were cutting up the flesh of a goat."

I dropped the phone and told my family that my brother had been murdered by those determined to stop me from ever going home.

"Which brother?" they asked.

I had only one brother.

As I went upstairs, my mind was flooded by images of blood, body parts, babies, screams, and bones. Nobody followed me as I climbed the stairs. I laid down on my bed and cried for hours.

When I finally got up the next day, I walked out of my house without saying a word to my family. Brittney caught up with me at the door and wanted to follow me out.

"Come back here," Brenda yelled at her.

"I am going to Madagascar with grandpa," Brittney said.

"Get your behind here, right now!" Brenda yelled.

The family watched me climb down the stairs with a traveling bag in tow. None of them tried to stop me. I got into my car and drove off. I drove eighteen miles to the Los Angeles Airport clutching my KLM ticket to Lagos before it occurred to me that I was two days ahead of my scheduled travel date.

As I made my way back to the parking lot, I saw Dr. Ikedife loading his luggage into his wife's car.

"Coming back from home?" I asked.

"Yes," he answered. "Like I told you, it was a quick visit. I said goodbye to my old man who is dying of prostate cancer."

"Sorry to hear that," I said.

"Oh, he is old now," Dr. Ikedife said. "And something will

always bring it to an end. If it is not cancer it will be something else."

For a moment, I missed my father. Maybe if he had lived longer, my life would have been different. Maybe I would have had more reason to get involved with activities at home earlier than now. Maybe Georgina would have persevered and given Nigeria another chance. Maybe my children would have had a reason to care about where I came from. I stopped myself from thinking how he would have viewed my present relationship with my family. In his world, a man was not supposed to be seen in the kitchen let alone be caught cooking. It would have been considered an abomination. In his world, a woman who refused to cook what a man wanted would dare not throw away a man's cooking. It would have been called a double abomination. My father would have considered my situation one in which dying would have been a better option.

"I can see you have your traveling bag, where to?" Dr. Ikedife asked me.

"I was scheduled to travel home in two days time but I came to the airport today"

"Everything alright?" Dr. Ikedife asked.

"My brother was hacked to death yesterday," I said.

"Oh my God!" he exclaimed.

"Don't say that!" Ikedife's wife said.

"Yes. Some political thugs murdered him," I said.

"Is it safe for you to go home then?" Dr. Ikedife asked.

"I don't know," I replied.

"You have to think about your safety before you rush home,"

he advised.

"The possibility of dying does not stop people from going to war," I quipped.

"But good warriors choose their battles carefully," Dr. Ikedife said.

"If I don't go now, I may never go home again," I said.

"You should go home and bury your brother."

"Yes, I will."

"But it needs to be planned."

"Yes."

"Did your wife know what happened?" Dr. Ikedife asked.

"I told her."

"And she allowed you to head home?"

"She does not care."

"I'm sorry to hear this."

"Such is life."

"I think you should come with us," Dr. Ikedife said. "Let us go to my house for a while."

"Ok," I accepted almost without thinking.

"When we get home, I will call my brother. I will ask him to provide you with military escort from the airport to anywhere you go in Nigeria," Dr. Ikedife said.

"Until when?" I asked.

"Until you enter the plane for your journey back to the United States" he assured.

I had wanted to tell him that I had planned on going for good, but I held myself in check. If he would not move back home with his brother in the military, he would consider me crazy for thinking that, I guessed. I felt crazy just thinking about it. How could I live with those savages? What kind of security guarantee would make me do it?

Dr Ikedife climbed into his wife's car. I opened the back door, tossed my bag on the seat and climbed in too, as airport security staff waved the car on.
"Something smells like *Ogiri* in this car," I said.
"I brought the original *ogiri okpi*," Dr. Ikedife said.
"Good," I said.
I closed my eyes and took in the aroma. My wandering brain stopped as soon as I made the concession. Home is not where you get back to. Home is where you are stuck.

Acknowledgements

Even though it was a last minute decision to put this book together in support of the "This America Sef Tour," it still requires an army of people to make it happen. It includes people who worked on the manuscript, people who picked up my slack at every other station of my life while I worked on the manuscript and those who were cheering from the side.

Amongst those who read the manuscript are Kwesi 'Jahbeloved' Baako, Margret Mukami Kamau and Chika Oduah. Your perspectives have helped in a long way to shape my vision.

Cheering on the side is Okey Ndibe. Ok, sometimes he cheers from the ring, too. Though this is not what you had in mind, 'but heck, a man got to do what a man got to do.'

I must express my gratitude to my tour partner, Adeola Fayehun. If you had not signed up for this tour, this book may still have remained one of the stillborn. Your drive is a source of strength to anyone privileged to work with you.

To all those who have published my works in different columns over the years, I say thank you- McLord Obiorah of Nigeria & Africa magazine, Moe Ene of Kwenu.com, Chuck Odili of Nigeriaworld.com, Adekunle Philips of

Nigeriavillagesquare.com, Alex Kabba of African-Abroad USA newspaper, Chido Nwangwu of USAfricaonline.com.

And of course, the big mogul himself, Omoyele Sowore of Saharareporters.com.

Some of the works in this book were once published in one form or the other by one or more of these chroniclers of our stories. They provided the vehicle that brought the tale to town.

I want to thank my wonderful mother-in-law, Gold Veronica Onwunyi, for being a wonderful mother to us all. She made it possible for me to disappear for a long time without wondering what happens to my two kids, Ijeamaka and Ogonna.

To my kids, Ijeamaka and Ogonna, thank you for understanding. Daddy is just trying to do better so that you will have a stronger shoulder to climb on.

To my beautiful wife, Edna: all these years, you have refused to be fatigued- not by dreams deferred, by promises unfulfilled or by follies enhanced by age. You are the editor-in-chief and the counselor-in-chief. You are more than everything.

And to all the people who have read and responded in one way or the other to anything I have written- please accept my appreciation.

About the Author

Rudolf Ogoo Okonkwo is a Nigerian journalist and writer. He is the host of the "Dr. Damages Show" on SaharaTV online. He also writes a weekly column, "Correct Me If I'm Right," for Saharareporters.com.

He has a Bachelor's degree in Engineering from the Federal University of Technology, Akure in Ondo State, Nigeria and an MFA in Professional and Creative Writing from Western Connecticut State University, Danbury, USA.

He is the author of a book of essays, "Children of A Retired God." A chapter of his memoir, "Because I'm my Grandfather," was a finalist in the 2010 John Guyon Literary Non-fiction Prize Competition. His short story, "The Butcher, the Surgeon & Me," was a finalist in Glimmer Train's 2009 Open Fiction Competition. He just finished work on his first novel, "Death on Mount Trashmore."